YOU TOO CAN BE A HOMEOWNER

SUCCESSFUL STRATEGIES TO NAVIGATE THE EMOTIONAL ROLLERCOASTER RIDE OF BECOMING A FIRST-TIME HOMEOWNER

Crystal Young, Esq

ISBN 978-1-7355260-3-4 (paperback)

JM Publishing

Printed in the United States of America

CONTENTS

ACKNOWLEDGMENT

To my parents, Arthur Young and Kathleen Young, who showed my brothers and I that we can achieve homeownership if we work hard and never give up. I love you Mom, Dad, Ivan, and Lamont.

To my publisher, best friend, and 4x best-selling author, Jermain Miller, who reminded me that everyone has a story if you just put paper to pen. Thanks for your coaching and encouragement throughout this process.

To my mentor, Raymond Suris, Esq., who not only pushed but assisted me in implementing a plan to purchase my first home. I will be forever grateful for you and owe much of my success to your guidance.

To all of the real estate professionals and homebuyers who have entrusted me with your transactions over the years. Thank You. You guys are all the real MVPs!

INTRODUCTION

Hello, my name is Crystal Young, and I am a real estate attorney in New York.

Growing up, I was raised by hard-working parents who put education first. My mom and dad provided everything for my two brothers and I even making sure our home was rezoned into one of the best school districts on Long Island. My parents' goal was to ensure we received the best education. As I entered my first year of middle school in sixth grade, I did not understand how instrumental this change would be for me. At eleven years old, I was focused on leaving my friends behind and the fear of starting a new school without knowing anyone. At the time, I was too young to consider that my new school district would expose me to a whole new world of opportunity that I may not have otherwise experienced. Thanks, Mom and Dad!

I discovered that the families in my new school district thought differently. They spoke of wealth, legacy, and homeownership. Through this exposure, I was driven at a young age to excel, in order to be in the same position. I watched my dad work two jobs while my mom worked from 4 pm to 12 am (even on the weekends). My parents did their absolute best to ensure we had a roof over our heads and the bills were paid. I got good grades in school and was accepted into my first choice of school: The University of Maryland at College Park. Go Terrapins! I majored in psychology, embarking on a journey to become a child psychiatrist.

I returned to New York after my second year of college. I did not want to leave Maryland, but my scholarships did not cover full out-of-state tuition, and the student loans were limited. I remember my parents refinancing their home to cover the balance during the second semester of my second year, just so I could register for classes. I did not want to place any more financial stress on them than they already had, so I came home after the summer of my second year intending to work, then apply to a State University of New York (SUNY) school for cheaper in-state tuition.

It did not happen (just yet.) Instead, I applied for a job in a retail store working some crazy hours and simultaneously received an offer to work at a law firm as a bookkeeper's assistant. For the eight years following, I worked both jobs: the retail job at night and weekends and the law firm gig from Monday through Friday (9-5 pm). When I decided to quit the retail job at the department store, a major cosmetics company contacted me to work as a makeup artist, traveling to various stores to do makeup on customers during special events. I thought it was an amazing opportunity, so I took the job while still employed at the law firm.

I was promoted several times at the law firm. From a bookkeeper's assistant to an assistant paralegal, to a paralegal, and eventually to a supervising paralegal. When the opportunity came for me to become a paralegal, the entire trajectory of my life was changed. As I assisted the attorneys at the firm and helped our clients with their legal transactions, I realized something: I loved helping people. From the customers I helped at the cosmetic company to the clients at the law firm, I truly loved helping others. After many years at the law firm, I felt that I hit a ceiling.

I wanted to be in control, more involved. I wanted to build a practice to assist my clients from start to finish. I also felt that I could give more in terms of service. So after eight years working at the law firm, I made the decision to apply to a State University of New York school to complete my bachelor's degree with every intention of going to law school.

I continued to work full-time at the law firm, part-time for the cosmetics brand (mostly weekend events), and attended school at night. I was so focused on my goal of becoming an attorney that I did not take the summers off. Now in my late twenties/early thirties, I wanted to complete school as quickly as possible. It was not the easiest path to get to my dreams, but no path ever is.

After graduating from law school, I wrote down my goals. My biggest goal was to show people that purchasing a home should not be a difficult process, particularly when working with an experienced attorney. Deciding to buy a home is one of the biggest decisions many individuals will make in their lifetime, and I wanted to play a major role in their decision.

Who would have known that after thousands of transactions and many success stories, I would find myself motivating clients every day? The initial dream of becoming a child psychiatrist had transformed into an undeniable passion for helping clients in one of the most important decisions they will make during their lifetime.

My role as a real estate attorney is to help my clients reach the goal of homeownership. My motto is, "You, too, can become a homeowner." I have the best seat in the house in that I get to witness our clients reach their goal and the role it plays for their future generation.

The fact that I am able to play such an important role in an individual or family's life is what really drives me to get up each morning. My purpose is to help my clients see the importance of homeownership, keep them focused on their goal, and assist in pulling them through any difficult situation they may face during the transaction.

There are a lot of reasons to become a homeowner. Unfortunately, some of us sit on the sidelines, waiting for that perfect opportunity to make a move for so long, that we never take any action. We watch everyone around us take steps to hit their goal of homeownership, but we are trapped in fear.

The purpose of this book is to educate homebuyers on the importance of homeownership and the process involved. When looking for an experienced attorney to be a part of your team, I want to be the one you work with! I want my clients to experience all the journey to homeownership has to offer in the most positive, liberating way possible. My number one goal is for my clients to have the greatest experience during their home buying process.

Over the years, I have been privileged to meet so many different people and help so many buyers, sellers, real estate agents, and mortgage brokers get to the closing table successfully. It would be my honor to work with you!

See you at the closing table!

CHAPTER 1

So, You Want to Purchase a Home. Now What?

Find Your Homeownership WHY

Purchasing a home is one of the biggest decisions anyone can make. But let's be real—life happens, and homeownership can quickly go from the top of your list to being replaced by all of the things you feel are more important. It happens more often than not, and we can find ourselves upset at the fact that we have not accomplished the goal we set for ourselves.

Over the years of representing thousands of amazing clients, I have come to realize that the people who buy homes have varying circumstances. However, their **WHY** to purchase a home outweighed any excuse.

The first step when purchasing a home is to find your **WHY.**

Here are some WHYs for many of my clients:

- Homeownership was a lifetime goal
- Getting married and want/need a bigger space for a family
- No longer want to pay their landlord's mortgage. (i.e., pay rent)
- Build wealth through an income-producing property to pass down to children for generations

One of the major reasons people fail to make it to the closing table is FEAR. I like to define FEAR in two ways: "Face everything and rise, or face everything and run." When you rise, you rise above all of the reasons why you shouldn't be a homeowner. When you run, you're running away from your WHY.

Fear can be paralyzing and cause us to give up on our goal and dream of homeownership. So we start to make excuses as to why it's not the right time to purchase a home. When fear starts to speak, it is important to remember why you really want to be a homeowner. There will be moments on the journey when you feel overwhelmed. This is when the WHY kicks in, and if it's well defined, it will pull you through when most people quit.

Wanting to purchase a home and actually being able to purchase one are two different things. First, you must be in the best position to get to the closing table. What does that mean? Well, you will not just wake up one day as a homeowner. You must follow a blueprint designed to get you there.

Your blueprint should look like this:

- Having a down payment
- Understanding your credit and its power
- Knowing what you can afford
- Researching the area you want to move to
- Defining the type of home you want
- Having the right team (which we will discuss later in the chapter)

Someone once said: "Luck is when opportunity meets preparation." If you are prepared when the opportunity presents itself, you will become a homeowner. Once you know why you want to own a home and conquer your fear, You, Too, Can Become a Homeowner. It's really that easy!

Don't Quit, You've Got This!

A recent client of mine, a single mom, experienced some personal challenges during her home buying process. After signing the contract and producing her down payment check, she questioned whether she wanted the home at all. My paralegal and I walked her through the process and addressed all her questions and concerns. Upon receipt of loan clearance from her chosen lender, we were thrilled to schedule the closing with her.

However, after we sent her the certified check amount required for her closing, she responded, "What if I do not show up?" I thought to myself, that is a unique question, because clients are usually relieved on closing day. After all, their homeownership pursuit is *finally* coming to an end. The day of closing is like the grand finale or crossing the finish line—it is a time for a celebration!

If she did not show up at the closing, she would be in default of the contract, putting her down payment at risk. Talk about a stressful situation for a homebuyer on closing day. After many years of handling real estate transactions, I knew there was something deeper than a refusal to appear at the closing. I believed she had become crippled by fear. Sometimes, when people become overwhelmed, they make decisions based on temporary emotions that have long-term effects. Some even blame the circumstances causing the fear on externals (i.e., the realtor, mortgage lender, inspector, Seller, the attorneys, and the weather), rather than taking a moment to determine the true cause of their fear, which is often a limited belief that they do not deserve or cannot maintain the home.

When I called her to discuss her reticence, I could hear the stress in her voice. It was almost as if her world had just come crashing down on what should be one of the most joyous days of her life! I listened to her concerns and explained her legal rights under the contract signed by both her and the Seller, three months prior. She understood that she would lose her down payment and said, "So be it."

After years of experiencing the ups and downs and roller-coaster of emotions a first-time homebuyer often encounters before closing, I knew she just needed a moment to think about the decision she was about to make.

I confirmed the conversation with our client in writing and called the Seller's attorney's office, indicating my client would not appear at the closing table. Immediately, the paralegal started to scream at me, reminding me that my client had signed a contract, and "She cannot do that."

When emotions are high, I know it's important to stay calm, and I understood how disappointed her Seller might feel. However, my role as the Purchaser's lawyer is to ensure I communicate my client's intent to the Seller's attorney and understand the legal ramifications of any action taken by my client and/or the Seller.

This took place all before 9 am on a Monday morning. Gotta love Mondays! The closing was set for noon, the same day.

I checked my email and discovered a response to my cancellation confirmation from my Purchaser client. The Purchaser responded, "I have two questions," so I immediately called her back.

I answered her questions, but she was still clearly stressed. So I shared some stories of other homebuyers I represented over the years, including my personal home buying story.

I went through these emotions when I purchased my first home as well, so I could certainly empathize. When buying my first home, my debt-to-income ratio was tight due to student loans. There were days that I was ecstatic that I would finally become a homeowner. But there were also days the lender would call me to discuss steps I needed to take to bring my debt-to-income ratio to a place that would allow for loan approval. These conversations with my lender would send me into a downward spiral of emotions. Many times throughout the process, I wanted to just throw in the towel.

When I finally received clearance to close from the lender and it was time to schedule the closing, I remember thinking, "How will I maintain a home as a single woman? What if I have a change of circumstance and cannot afford the mortgage? Who will help me? What would I do if the pipes froze?" (which actually happened a month after my closing, so I called a plumber.) Since I went through the homeownership process and all of these emotions myself, I can better help my clients understand and sort out their own concerns. It probably also helps that I was a psychology major. Mom would be proud I actually got to use my psychology degree.

I told my client another story of a Purchaser I represented who was afraid to put money down for the contractual deposit. She refused to wire the money to the Seller's counsel out of fear, even once I explained that it would be held in the Seller's attorney's trusted escrow account. "If he spends your money, he will lose his license," I reminded her. When given other options to tender the contractual deposit, she did not want to obtain a certified check from the bank and did not have a personal checkbook. She tried everything that might explain why she would not tender the contractual deposit. Finally, after many hours over several weeks explaining the importance of the deposit and why it is necessary to secure the transaction, she decided to move forward and agreed to hand deliver a check to the Seller's attorney's office. Unfortunately, however, the Seller had already moved forward with a contract with a different Purchaser (who quickly tendered their contractual deposit), and our Purchaser was left devastated. She attributed her fear of change to causing her to lose the house of her dreams.

I explained that every client experiences different emotions throughout their home buying journey, but the hard part is over, and today should be a happy day for my client and her family. At noon, she would sign the mortgage and title documents and receive a copy of the deed, while I sit with her every step of the way. After that, the keys to the home will be handed over for her to immediately move in with her family.

By the end of the conversation, I reminded the Purchaser that I already notified the Seller's counsel, the title company, and the lender's counsel that she would not be in attendance at the closing table. If she decided to change her mind, it must be well before the 12 pm closing (it was about 9:30 am by then). I also assured her that she was not immune to this rollercoaster of emotions, as some Purchasers experienced last-minute doubts when purchasing their first home.

Before I could end the call, she said: "Crystal, call them back. I want to move forward. See you at twelve pm!" This was a beautiful end to what could have been a not-so-happy day for our Purchaser and her family.

There are some valuable lessons a Purchaser gains during the home buying process. Many of our clients learn how they react to challenging situations. Some get overwhelmed and want to give up, while others push towards their end goal no matter what personal challenges they are faced with throughout the journey.

I once represented a Purchaser who was faced with an open permit on the property. The Seller took action with the town to close out the permit but could not get it done prior to closing due to a nationwide pandemic. Instead of throwing in the towel or becoming agitated at a circumstance beyond her control, she contacted me to determine her liabilities and responsibilities if she were to close with open permits on the property. She asked a lot of questions to be thoroughly informed before making a decision. In the end, she decided to close before the Seller's closure of the permits. The Seller's attorney held back a significant sum in his escrow account to ensure the Seller completed his responsibilities after closing. If the Seller failed to do so, the sum would be released to my client, and she was quite okay with that. In this case, the Seller was able to close the permit within 60 days of the closing date, and all parties were satisfied.

The end goal and its gratification are much greater than the challenge faced.

Someone once said, "A positive attitude gives you power over your circumstances instead of your circumstances having power over you." Carry this idea with you, along with your WHY, during your homeownership journey. You will be unstoppable.

Sometimes, when one is at the finish line, the challenge feels increasingly greater towards the end. My role as an attorney is not to push my client one way or the other but to protect their interests throughout the process. When representing a Purchaser, I must ensure my client understands the provisions of their contract of sale, including their rights and responsibilities when purchasing a home. Additionally, I must be sure they understand both the title and mortgage process and meet all deadlines required under the contract of sale. Setting expectations is key when representing a Purchaser as, most often, it is their first time engaging in the home buying process. My role is to guide the Purchaser through closing and ultimately establish a smooth closing table experience.

There has been tension at closing tables simply because Purchasers and Sellers were upset over an uncontrollable closing delay. Near the finish line, emotions are sometimes high. However, if you are laser-focused on your WHY of homeownership, your experience will be different, and nothing will stop you from achieving your goal.

Your Championship Team

Winning a championship in any sport requires a great coach and a team that understands the journey. It also takes sacrifices and dedication by the players. The championship, in this case, is homeownership. You will not want to let your team (family), coach (attorney, mortgage professional, realtor), or, most importantly, yourself down.

There are many elements that come into play during the home buying process, which we will discuss and cover throughout this book. By far, the most important factor is your TEAM. Yes, you bet—in this case, teamwork really does make the dream work. You need a great team to ensure you are executing at a high level and getting the results you desire. If you want your transaction to run smoothly, you need a team of experienced professionals on your side.

You need to work with people who have your best interests in mind. A great team consists of a reliable support system that includes your real estate professional, attorney (me), mortgage broker, home inspector, friends and family that support you, and a positive mindset so that whatever challenges you may face throughout the transaction, you can face it with grace, class and undeniable perseverance!

Remember to take advice only from trusted individuals on your team. Even though your family and friends will have your best interests in mind, they may unintentionally give you bad advice. For example, I worked with a couple who were first-time homebuyers. When applying for a mortgage loan, they realized that they needed an extra $5,000 to cover closing costs. They asked one of their family members who told them they could apply for a personal loan through a credit union. Without speaking with their mortgage lender, they took the advice of the family member and applied for the loan. Though they were approved for the

$5,000 personal loan, the credit inquiry caused their credit to drop significantly and debt-to-income ratio to increase. Thereby, their mortgage application was denied, and they lost the home. Apparently, the family member had never bought a home and indicated he "figured that would get them the money they needed to close." So the lesson here is two-fold: Do not take advice from someone that has not purchased a home themselves AND avoid any action that can affect your credit, debt-to-income ratio, or income once you are pre-approved for a mortgage loan.

In preparation for your home buying journey, here are some questions that you should answer that can help facilitate your home buying experience.

1. Make a list of goals for your home buying journey. What are you looking for?
2. What is your WHY for buying a home?
3. What does your home buying blueprint look like?
4. What team have you assembled to assist you in finding a home?
5. What factors do you need to focus on, to help your home buying experience run smoothly?

CHAPTER 2

The Start of the Home Buying Process

Getting Organized

Buying a home requires a lot of time and effort. It can seem like a full-time job. The easiest way to avoid working another job to become a homeowner is by first getting organized. When I say organized, I mean start writing out a list of goals in the order of their importance!

There are lots of moving parts to think about when you are looking for a new home. Begin researching early to uncover what you desire the most in a home. Ask yourself:

- What type of home do I want to live in?
- What are the benefits/costs of living there?

- ❖ Is it in close proximity to work/school/public transportation?
- ❖ Does it fit my family?

There are many things to consider when determining the best home for you and your family. Ensuring that you stay organized during the process will result in the best possible outcome.

Make a note of certain homes you are interested in and pay attention to how long the home remains on the market. In many cases, houses in "hot markets" do not remain available for long. Therefore, it is crucial to be well prepared to make a quick offer before your competition prevails.

You want to connect with an experienced realtor who has the knowledge of the market and the professionalism to submit a well-drafted offer. You also want to connect with a mortgage professional who will provide a pre-approval indicating how much house you are eligible to buy based on your income, the taxes on the property, and other loan terms or individual factors.

Often, due to our financial circumstances, we must categorize our dream home in our dream location as something that we will work towards in the future. Your present circumstance (based on the pre-approval provided by your lender) may require you to look in different areas and at another price point. One thing is for certain, you MUST remain open to possibilities. Sometimes this is a tough pill to swallow. Acknowledge that you qualify to purchase a home, but not in the exact area you desire, JUST YET.

Read that again. I said "just yet" because I want you to know that, in due time, you can accomplish anything you put your mind to.

Keep in mind, your first home may not be your dream home, and that's okay! It could become your investment property, thereby placing you in an even better position overall to purchase a dream home.

I have certainly watched first-time homebuyers purchase their dream home as their first home. I have also witnessed our first-time homebuyers purchase what we call a "starter home," which needs lots of renovation. After some years, they pull out the equity in the home, find a tenant to rent the home, and purchase their dream home. There are so many opportunities associated with homeownership if you make a move and stay organized by knowing the costs of maintaining the home and deciding what is best for you and your family.

I love seeing my clients feel a sense of relief and accomplishment, and it means so much to guide them to the closing table. After all, they stayed organized and followed the steps to homeownership. Once you do something for the first time (and especially something as big as purchasing a home), you typically believe that you are capable of doing it again. That is the remarkable thing about having goals and accomplishing them. It's possible for you to be a homeowner and believe that you can do it again—and again, and again.

Remember that staying organized is one of the most important things you can do during your journey towards homeownership.

Hiring the Right Realtor

When purchasing your first home, it is a very good idea to work with a realtor. The realtor acts as your representative when looking for homes by helping you narrow down your search, in accordance with the availability of homes on the market and the terms of your pre-approval. In addition, the realtor often has access to databases that reflect homes that have not even hit the public yet. Your real estate agent is also hired to submit a professional offer to the Seller or listing agent, which, if submitted outside of a real estate agent, may not stand a chance of acceptance (due to missing information or lack of knowledge of proper offer submission etiquette). Finally, your realtor has often represented hundreds of clients, which allows them to keep you informed and stress-free during the search for your new home.

In speaking with a recent client, she mentioned how it took her two years to find a property. She had decided to work without a realtor, thinking it would save her time and money and allow her to control when she wanted to look at properties. These were good reasons, but she also underbid in hot markets and, in some cases, took too long to submit offers because she wanted to think about it. Looking back, she cringed at how many properties she had really loved but lost by initially not wanting to work with a realtor.

Your realtor is one of the most important team members you can have when purchasing a home. Therefore, it is important to choose the right realtor to help you get through the process. An experienced realtor can introduce you to great mortgage lenders, attorneys, and inspectors. They can provide you with helpful information so you do not overpay for your new home. Their knowledge of the home buying process, negotiation skills, and connection to the brokerage community can be extremely beneficial for you. Especially when multiple offers are on the table for a home you absolutely adore.

The right realtor will make sure you receive the best outcome and ensure that you and your family get to the closing table. You can also ask for a referral from a trusted friend or family member who recently purchased a home. *Recently* is key. Please do not ask grandma about her experience in purchasing her home fifty-nine years ago. The process of the transaction may be very different from the way things are done now.

While I hear stories all the time, one stuck out most. A new Purchaser was purchasing a condo in the city at a new development. He loved the property; it was spacious, brand new, had great upside potential, and the location was exactly where he wanted to be, a short distance to work and nightlife. The realtor was able to negotiate a great price as well as concessions, and the contracts were sent out. Although young and savvy, the Purchaser would not take advice from anyone except his mom. The Purchaser's mom felt the property should cost less and more concessions should be added. Mom mentioned she was able to get her home in the country this way, years ago. The Purchaser did not want to disappoint his mom, so he asked the realtor to resubmit the terms, which ultimately caused him to lose the home. Years later, while at a closing on another home, he reflected on that time and how the property value increased by three million dollars in a few short years. He wished he just told his mom he respected her input, but really wanted the house and would move forward with it. In this case, his realtor knew best.

Realtor referrals are a good option because you have a warm introduction to the real estate agent by someone you know and trust, who can often vouch for their work.

If you do not know of any good realtors, do an internet search for "best realtor in ___ (specific area)." You may want to post an inquiry on social media as well. Read their reviews. What are their clients saying about them? Do not get caught working with someone that does not match your energy and personality type, as you will be in the presence of this individual until you find your new home (which could be months). You want to feel comfortable with your real estate agent. You create your team, so choose wisely. This goes for your entire team, including the attorney, mortgage professional, etc.

When you work with a real estate agent, remember to find one who has a proven track record of closing transactions and is well-versed in the areas you are looking in (or at the very least willing to learn and do the research.) If the realtor resides in the area you wish to live in, even better! The agent will have firsthand experience and knowledge of the area and can provide insight to help you determine if it would be a good neighborhood and home for you and your family.

After speaking with a new homeowner recently, I asked about her experience with her agent. She stated, "Though my realtor is younger than me, I was able to trust him because real estate is his specialty."

In this case, the homeowner indicated that her realtor provided honest feedback about the current real estate market trends, which allowed her offer to be accepted. For example, the house was worth $550,000.00 in accordance with a market analysis containing the latest sales for similar properties, as examined by her realtor. The homeowner wanted to offer $500,000.00 ($50k less than the market value of a home this size). Her agent was very transparent and explained what it means to be in a "Seller's market." In a Seller's market, demand for homes exceeds supply. Thereby, Sellers are typically at an advantage as a Purchaser may offer the Seller's asking price or over the asking price, to win the bid. Often, there is competitive bidding in a Seller's market, and a potential Purchaser must submit their highest and best offer to even be considered amongst other bids. In this case, the realtor reminded her that an offer of $50k under the listed price of the home would most likely not be considered, and if this is a home she really desires, an offer at asking would most likely win the bid. The homeowner trusted her realtor and agreed to submit an offer at the listed price. Though there were several other offers at the list price, she won the bid, and we celebrated her success at the closing table. This homebuyer attributed her new home to the experience and professionalism of her real estate agent.

You want to feel secure that your realtor will best represent you as their client. Therefore, it is vital to establish trust at the onset of your homeownership journey.

A good agent will provide calm during the storm. Preferably, the realtor has a wide range of experience and will not panic if things should go awry (which happens more than we like to think). An experienced realtor will walk you through the process and provide you with solid advice.

A realtor friend once told me a story explaining how experience in hot markets pays off. He secured an appointment with a listing agent to show his clients a home. The Purchasers wanted the home, but wanted to take some time to think about it. The realtor explained why the sale could become a bidding war, and being the first offer shows how serious they are. The home was in a highly sought after community and was in pristine condition. The realtor explained to his Purchaser clients why it was important to submit a higher than asking price offer, immediately, if they wanted to secure this home. He also explained it was important to be the first offer and be the best. Waiting for other offers to come in, could require them to overbid or completely lose the home they truly wanted. Ultimately, they trusted the realtor's advice and offered slightly above the asking price. While multiple offers were presented on the home, the Purchasers won the bidding war and secured the home.

It is extremely important to have patience with yourself while your real estate agent and your team are working with you, towards your goal of homeownership. Sometimes you can come across a home you like, but your offer may not be accepted. Nobody likes rejection, and you may end up feeling discouraged. I always tell my clients to "trust the process" and believe the right house will find its way to them. However, you must continue to take action and never give up. The right home may have not hit the market, as yet. Don't despair, though; you have already gotten this far.

Your realtor is like your sounding board and will not leave your side until the house you are meant to own appears!

These are a few reasons why it's important to get organized and hire a realtor—not just any realtor, but the RIGHT realtor for you and your family.

Below are some questions that will help you in your search for the right home and realtor.

1. Why is it important to hire a real estate agent?
2. What qualities should you look for in a real estate agent?
3. Should you remain open to other locations when looking for a home? If so, why?
4. Is it okay to purchase a "starter" home now but look to buy a dream home in the future?

CHAPTER 3

Don't Go Shopping with a Hole in Your Bag

Know Who and What You're Working With

So, you are serious about purchasing a home. I know this because you are reading this book. I encourage you to take a moment and show yourself gratitude for taking this major step!

First, you hired a realtor, and now you need a mortgage professional/lender/broker.

Referrals are the preferred option when seeking a mortgage professional. You want to work with an experienced and recommended financial professional as you navigate purchasing your first home.

You can research and hire a mortgage professional before hiring your real estate agent or vice versa. Some first-time homebuyers prefer to ask their realtor or attorney to refer them to a mortgage professional whom they know, trust and have done business with in the past. It is important to connect with a team of professionals who know and trust others in their respective fields. You may find that your closing will flow seamlessly when you work with a group of professionals who are familiar with each other.

Remember to hire a mortgage professional at the onset of the transaction, as you will need a mortgage pre-approval letter. This is often a requirement of a realtor before taking you out to look for homes. For example, suppose you are approved for a mortgage of $200,000.00 and have a 3.5% down payment available. In that case, your realtor will not take you to homes worth over a million dollars. This is because homes of that price would be out of your purchasing power range at the moment, and the realtor does not want to waste your time forwarding properties that you are currently unable to purchase. An experienced realtor will always keep your best interests and expectations in mind when introducing properties to you.

Now, you might be thinking, what is a mortgage pre-approval letter?

A mortgage pre-approval letter is a statement from a lender that indicates you are qualified for a mortgage loan (upon satisfaction of certain conditions). It allows you to borrow up to a certain amount of money from a bank to purchase your new home. A mortgage pre-approval also provides the interest rate upon which you qualify at the time. After you identify a home, sign a contract, and your lender completes an appraisal, you will have the option to lock your rate through closing. Note that this interest rate is only good for a limited time and will eventually expire.

When a Purchaser locks their mortgage rate with the lender, this means the rate will remain the same until a time specified by the lender. The idea is for the rate to stay good through the closing date, so it is important to advise your lender of the last anticipated closing date as specified in your contract and request that your rate is locked through that date.

Though you can extend your rate once locked, you generally pay extension fees to retain the same rate, as rates fluctuate over time.

The mortgage pre-approval letter will give you an idea of where you are financially and what you can afford at the moment. Lenders have a wide range of competitively priced loan programs, particularly for first-time homebuyers. Ask your lender about loan programs for first-time homebuyers and special programs if you are a veteran or in the service industry (i.e., nurse, police officer, teacher). Also, take the time to research programs on your own and ask your mortgage lender if they can offer those rates and programs specific to your personal needs.

To determine the loan amount you may qualify for, a lender will gather all of your financial information from bank statements to tax returns, credit reports, debt-to-income ratio, and often rental history to provide a proposed loan amount and mortgage rate. Be sure to have all of your financial information readily available before speaking with your lender. Then, you can determine if this rate falls in line with your desired mortgage payment range, among other home buying goals.

Even if you personally feel that you need to save more money or have a certain credit score to purchase a home, speak with a lender. You may be pleasantly surprised to hear that you are in a better position than you originally thought, in qualifying for a mortgage loan.

Keep in mind, the better your financial situation, the more you may qualify for. However, just because you qualify for it does not mean you must use the full loan amount when looking for a home. If you find your desired home for less money than you need from a lender, even better.

Every homebuyer has their own priorities when choosing a mortgage. Some are interested in keeping their monthly payments low, while others want to ensure the loan is paid off in the least amount of time possible. Many Purchasers apply for a fixed-rate loan that ensures their principal and interest payments never increase. In contrast, there are various other loan products that may be favorable depending on a homebuyer's personal circumstances.

Remember, the mortgage pre-approval step is of utmost importance. If this step is neglected, you may be shopping with a hole in your bag.

What I mean is, when you find your dream home, you may lose it because you cannot make an immediate offer. If you are not pre-approved, then each time you find a home with potential, you have to go back to speak to your lender to see if you can afford it. This is not ideal when searching for a home and may ultimately cause you to lose time and, more importantly, the home. Do not allow this to happen to you. A prepared Purchaser immediately makes an offer that is accepted. There is no time to fuss around in a hot market. Time is not on your side when multiple Purchasers are competing for the home and offering an over-the-list price to set themselves apart, to win the bid.

Very rarely will an experienced realtor show properties without having a picture of what a Purchaser can afford. This is because your realtor does not want to waste your time and create a potentially heartbreaking situation when all of your offers are rejected. Rather, a good realtor will keep their client's needs and means in mind at all times, and make sure you can afford the homes they bring to the table.

When you have a mortgage pre-approval, it puts you in the driver's seat. It makes you an attractive Purchaser, especially in a Seller's market (when demand exceeds supply).

Be Attractive to Win

Depending on where you live in the country, it can take about 60 to 90 days, more or less, to close on a home. Though circumstances vary, the most significant delay is often caused by the time it takes to receive mortgage approval. However, you can certainly speed up the process and get to the closing table earlier than you might have otherwise, if you stay organized and understand the home buying process.

Having a pre-approval from a reputable lender makes a homebuyer extremely attractive and puts you ahead of the game. Notice I said reputable. If you obtain a pre-approval from an unknown online mortgage bank, the Seller may reject your offer, as they are unable to verify if the pre-approval is legit or valid.

A pre-approval from a reputable mortgage lender allows you to show the Seller you mean business and this is the house you really want. You are clear that you are not here to waste your time or theirs, and you are prepared to enter into a contract as soon as possible.

In my years in real estate, I have witnessed Purchasers who have missed out on dozens of homes. They had the down payment monies readily available, but they did not qualify for a mortgage due to credit issues, a significant debt-to-income ratio, or the like. Listen to your experienced realtor and ask for their honest advice when searching for a home. Your realtor knows the market and will be able to give valuable feedback concerning the homes available in your price range in accordance with the pre-approval letter provided.

There is nothing more heartbreaking than putting an offer in on a home and losing it because the other Purchaser had their pre-approval ready to present at the time of offer submission. A Seller and/or their agent (called the "listing agent") will want to feel comfortable that you are eligible for a mortgage and ready to move forward the moment the offer is accepted. There is no time to waste in real estate.

Before we move on to the next chapter, I want to stress again that just because you are pre-approved to borrow up to a certain loan amount, it does not mean you should borrow that full amount.

Homebuyers purchasing more than they can afford and overextending themselves was one of the major reasons for the housing crisis in 2008. It resulted in families losing homes that were backed with unsustainable mortgages. Trust your experienced real estate professionals to guide you while also deciding what is best for you and your family when purchasing a home.

Answer the questions below to ensure you are an attractively smart Purchaser:

1. Where do I obtain a mortgage pre-approval letter, and why is it important?
2. What financial information will a lender need to review before issuing a mortgage pre-approval letter?
3. What does it mean to shop with a hole in your bag?
4. Review your goals for the home buying process (Chapter 1). Are you making progress toward them?

CHAPTER 4

It's Time to Present an Offer

Make Your Goals Reality

After you identify the home in line with your goals, it's time to present an offer! Making an offer is an exciting and essential step to purchasing the home you desire, and understanding the process of presenting an offer on a home you want is extremely important. If this is the home that you truly want, you must be in the best possible position to acquire it. Your realtor is fully equipped and experienced in making an offer, to secure the home you love. However, you should also understand the information your realtor provides that will help your offer get accepted.

There are a few things Purchasers must take into consideration in order to present the strongest possible offer to a Seller and/or listing agent.

When purchasing a home, you should do research and communicate with your realtor to see what the current market trends are. When researching, check out the most recent homes in contract as well as the most recent sales in the area on comparable homes. You can go back as far as six months. This is important before you make an offer. If it is a Seller's market, you may hear that Purchasers are making offers close to or at the list price (even over the list price) and placing more money down at contract signing. This will make you competitive and quite possibly avoid bidding wars, but it does not guarantee your offer will be accepted.

Over the years, I have witnessed first-time homebuyers make offers up to $100k + over the Seller's asking price. This often occurs in a competitive market where there are multiple offers and motivated Purchasers who sometimes (but not always), have a significant down payment. If the purchaser applies for a mortgage, the lender will order an appraisal of the property. Often, the appraisal is returned at the Seller's original asking price, which may be significantly less than the contractual purchase price (the price originally offered by the Purchaser).

I once represented a Purchaser who offered $600,000.00 for a property listed by the Seller for $500,000.00. The

Seller knew the property was not worth $600,000.00, so he informed the Purchaser that he would only accept his offer if he waived any mortgage contingency or appraisal clauses in the contract. In other words, the Purchaser would agree to purchase the property notwithstanding the results of the appraisal.

An appraisal is an estimate of the property's current market value and is determined by a licensed appraiser. The appraiser reviews the recent sales of similar homes in the area based on the square footage of the home, number of bedrooms, bathrooms, etc., and assigns a value to the home. The appraiser then communicates this value to the lender, who will determine if the Purchaser is paying fair value for the home. The mortgage lender will not loan more than what the property is worth, so if the home does not appraise for the contractual purchase price AND there is a mortgage contingency clause in the contract (without any appraisal waivers), there are several options available to the Purchaser:

1. Ask the Seller to reduce the contractual purchase price to the appraised value. If the Seller agrees to reduce the purchase price, the Purchaser must proceed to closing with the new price.

2. The Seller may agree to reduce the purchase price, but not completely to the full appraised value of the property. The Purchaser can then decide if they wish to move forward with the new price, acknowledging that the Purchaser must pay the difference between the new contract price and the appraised value.
3. The Seller may refuse to reduce the contractual purchase price completely, notwithstanding the results of the appraisal. If there is a mortgage contingency clause in your contract, this will allow for either a cancellation of the contract or the Purchaser can choose to pay the difference between the new contract price and the appraised value.

I informed my client what waiving an appraisal contingency would mean for him financially and legally. This means that nothwithstanding the amount the home appraises for, the Purchaser would be bound to purchase it at the contract price. Options 1, 2, and 3 are not available if the Purchaser waives the appraisal and/or mortgage contingency provision in the contract.

The Purchaser applied for a mortgage with a reputable lender who ordered an appraisal to be completed on the property. The appraisal was returned at the Seller's list price of $500,000.00, which is $100,000.00 less than the contractual purchase price. The Purchaser was not surprised in this case because he offered $100,000.00 over the list price and waived the appraisal contingency. Thereby, the lender loaned him $100,000.00 less than what he was originally eligible for, and the Purchaser was required to come to closing with the extra $100,000.00 plus all closing costs.

As a real estate attorney, this is not something I would ever suggest to my client. However, your circumstance might be unique and in a Seller's market, it may be the only way to get the deal done. In this case, the Purchaser was relocating to New York for an employer who was footing the bill. This is certainly a unique situation, and all parties were able to close without any uncertainty or regrets.

In a Purchaser's market, however, the ball is in your court. In this market type, Sellers want to sell, and there are just not enough Purchasers. Thereby, the Seller may be more flexible in accepting provisions such as a Seller's concession, minimal down payment, and extended mortgage contingency deadlines or closing dates. If the home has been on the market for some time, presenting a low offer may not be a bad thing. However, if your offer is low, be sure you can back it up with comparable sales in the area on like properties. It is quite possible the house has remained on the market for an extended period of time because it is indeed overpriced.

Now that you have your pre-approval on hand and hired your realtor, you are one step closer to getting an accepted offer! To ensure this happens, it's important that you do the following:

Make sure the home is not only the house you WANT but also the one you can AFFORD.

Remember, the house you can afford is up to you (and the details of your pre-approval, of course).

Know Your Contingencies

Contingency clauses must be placed in the contract to protect the Purchaser (or Seller) in the transaction. The purpose of a contingency is to ensure that a party to the transaction (Purchaser or Seller) will not be required to close on the home or be held in default of the contract if a certain condition is not met. If the condition is not met, the Purchaser can cancel the contract and receive the return of their down payment without penalty and/or legal consequences.

It is crucial to discuss this with your realtor before placing your offer. The last thing you want to do is blindside your Seller with an additional contingency after your offer has been accepted. The Seller may believe that you are hiding something, playing games, or did this intentionally to delay the transaction. If the Seller thinks you are not trustworthy and withholding information (such as the requirement to sell your primary residence prior to closing), they may refuse to sign the contract and accept another eligible Purchaser's offer.

Here are five very important contingencies you should consider when making an offer on a home and before contract signing:

- ❖ Home Inspection
- ❖ Appraisal
- ❖ Clear Title
- ❖ Financing
- ❖ Home Sale

There is much more at risk for the Seller when it comes to contingencies. Often, the Seller does not feel secure in the transaction if too many or certain requested contingencies could allow the Purchaser an opportunity to cancel the transaction.

Waiving certain contingencies can make your offer more competitive, particularly in a Seller's market.

I want to reiterate that I do not recommend waiving contingency clauses in the contract. However, your personal and unique situation may require and/or allow for this. If so, you absolutely must speak with your real estate agent and attorney to fully understand what is at stake when you waive a contingency.

I will further discuss contract contingencies and their importance in Chapter 6… stick with me!

You Put the Offer In, Now What?

After you or your realtor have submitted your offer, the Seller has a decision to make. It's simple: accept it, reject it, or respond with what is called a counteroffer.

If your realtor receives a counteroffer, the Seller wants to negotiate and typically has a purchase price in mind. If presented with a counteroffer, you can decide if you want to accept, reject it or counter the counteroffer.. If your counter is rejected, the Seller may continue to list the home or accept another offer.

If the Seller does not present a counteroffer, you, as the Purchaser, can decide to accept the purchase price, reject it, or perhaps increase your offer to a number close to what the Seller wants and/or waive contingencies. Keep in mind, you can typically negotiate more than just the price.

For example, suppose you know your Seller wants a quick closing date. In that case, you can agree the appraisal will be completed in 14 days with a mortgage commitment letter within 30 days (instead of 45). Perhaps you can even push up the closing date. However, before making any promises, be sure this is possible with your lender and attorney, as you do not want to place yourself in an unfavorable predicament. Do not make unrealistic promises in your offer as an experienced Seller and/or listing agent will know you are blowing smoke, as they say.

It is important to have your dream team in place at the onset of the transaction. You want to lean on your team to help guide you through each stage of your homeownership journey. You must be clear on what your options are to secure your home. If it comes down to the purchase price and you have a max price in mind, it is vital to have this discussion with your realtor. An experienced realtor will explain the best steps to take to ensure you secure a home within your budget.

Do not be surprised if you and the Seller (through your respective real estate agents) go back and forth on even a few hundred dollars to get to a final number both sides will be comfortable with. Often, the listing agent will ask for your "best and final offer" before making a decision. If the Seller rejects your offer, it is time to get back in the game and start looking for another property. This is not the time to feel defeated or discouraged and give up. You absolutely must keep the momentum going. Keep a positive mindset and trust in the process. Tell yourself, "My offer will be accepted on the house that is meant for me," and trust this will be the case.

After being outbid on a few properties and having all the reason to be discouraged, a recent client refused to give up. He was determined to find the right property at the right price. Finally, not only was he able to secure the right property, but it was on the same block where he lost two other properties in bidding wars. There were some issues with this property that other Purchasers were unwilling to take on, but my client understood the true value of the property. The Seller wanted to close fast and knew the house needed significant repair, therefore, the Seller agreed to the lower price just to move forward quickly. My client purchased the home for $200,000 less than the asking price and only spent $30k in renovations. A year later and he has over $200k in equity in the property due to his patience and perseverance

After the closing, I always ask my clients about their home buying journey. They are often grateful that the offer on the first or second home was not accepted because they just closed on the perfect home for them and their family. You may have to go through a few of these challenges to get to the right home. Remember, however, that these experiences can help you with your next offer on the new property. If the Seller rejects your first offer, do not feel defeated! You are learning the process and are just one more step closer to the closing table.

Once the right offer is accepted by the Seller, it's now time for you to hire a licensed home inspector and begin contract review with your attorney.

Before moving forward, answer the questions below to give you the greatest advantage of submitting the best offer:

1. What should you take into consideration to present the strongest offer?
2. What should you do if the Seller presents a counteroffer?
3. What are five contingencies you should consider when making an offer on a home?
4. What is the next step once your offer is accepted?

CHAPTER 5

Home Inspections: Do You Need One?

The Importance of a Home Inspection

Out of all the steps in your homeownership journey, the home inspection is one of the most important.

After your offer is accepted by the Seller, you should contact a licensed home inspector who will examine the property and determine if it is structurally sound. The inspector will provide a detailed description of any major or minor issues with the premises and typically produce a written report to the Purchaser within 48 hours of the inspection.

Often, the home inspector will allow you to walk through the premises with them and point out items that may need repair either immediately or in the distant future. I encourage you to take this opportunity to watch what the inspector does to assess the working condition of the heating and air conditioning systems, plumbing, electrical systems, and appliances, as you will have an opportunity to complete a second inspection on the day of the closing. This is called a "walk-through" of the premises.

Once you receive the inspection report, do not panic! The inspection report may contain page after page (pictures and written descriptions) of suggested repairs and structural or cosmetic defects, which, if left incomplete, would not significantly change the value of the property.

I often speak with a Purchaser after the inspection, and I am informed that the Purchaser wants every single item raised in the inspection report resolved by the Seller prior to closing. After first confirming the true intentions of the Seller with the realtor, I have to remind the Purchaser that the home was placed on the market with the consideration that the purchase price reflects the true value of the property before repairs. However, there are some circumstances where the Seller will agree to all or some of the repairs. It really depends on the Seller and their expectations when initially placing the home on the market. Typically, the Seller does not list their property to build a brand new one for sale. This is important to remember when reviewing the inspection report.

Over the years, I have experienced many instances where the Purchaser lost the property due to unreasonable repair requests. In a competitive market, most Sellers understand they can sell their home "as is" without making any repairs to the property. Some Sellers take it personally when the Purchaser submits a list of repairs, especially when deemed minor in the eyes of the Seller. Always speak with your real estate agent to determine what repairs and/or credits should be requested, if any, based on the offer submitted, comparable sales, condition of the property, and information provided by the listing agent concerning the Seller's intentions.

Suppose the parties agree to allow an inspection after contract signing. In that case, there must be an inspection clause in the contract, allowing the purchaser to cancel the contract and receive the return of their contractual down payment if they are not satisfied with the condition of the home. In many cases, and depending on what is customary in your region, the home inspection is completed *prior* to signing the contract—allowing you to negotiate repairs as part of the contract review process and/or request a credit at closing or a reduction of the purchase price before signing the contract.

Depending on the state where you are purchasing the property and the type of home you are purchasing, inspection costs may vary. No matter the cost, it is extremely important to hire a licensed inspector when purchasing a home. You certainly would hate to discover a material defect in the six-figure home you just bought that could have been discovered during an $800 inspection. When purchasing a home, you want to evaluate the costs/benefits of your decisions throughout the process. If you are unsure at any point in the process, I encourage you to speak with your team of professionals for direction.

A home inspection can reveal whether the electrical, plumbing, and other major structures were installed to code. If there are crossed and double-tapped wires, for example, these items can be deemed a fire hazard. When reviewing the inspection report, look for any imminent hazards and request their repair before closing. It is important to note that your lender will order an appraisal of the premises once the contract is fully executed by both parties. If the appraiser discovers any potential dangers, such as missing staircase railings or broken steps, the lender will be notified and require the items to be repaired before the issuance of loan clearance to schedule a closing.

Alternatively, the Seller may allow the Purchaser to make the repair at the Purchaser's costs.

Your real estate contract should contain a provision regarding repairs as it pertains to lender approval. Should the lender require repairs on the premises, there are generally three options for the Seller:

1. The Seller can agree to complete the repairs necessary to satisfy the Purchaser's mortgage lender. The repairs must be completed before the loan is approved, and an inspector hired by the lender must revisit the property to confirm the repairs were completed to the satisfaction of the lender.
2. The Seller may allow the Purchaser to hire a licensed professional to complete the repairs on the Seller's behalf. As in #1, the repairs must be completed before the loan is approved, and an inspector hired by the lender must revisit the property to confirm the repairs were completed to the satisfaction of the lender.
3. The Seller can decide they do not want repairs to be completed on the property. In this case, the

mortgage loan will be denied, and the Purchaser will receive the full return of the down payment. The contract will be canceled, and the Purchaser can seek other homes.

If there is an illegal room (i.e., full kitchen) in the basement of a home without the proper permit, certificate of occupancy, and egress windows for safety, the Purchaser's lender may deny the loan or delay issuance of loan clearance until said appliance/structure is installed or removed. For instance, a finished basement with a bathroom may be required to be converted back to its original condition for loan approval. Otherwise, the Purchaser may be burdened with costly expenses for permits, new architectural drawings, and renovations after closing. In the alternative, many lenders are not concerned with these matters so always consult with your mortgage professional as these matters arise.

When making an offer on the property, ask if the home has all the proper permits and certificates of occupancy, which essentially reflect the legal status of the home and all structures on the property. In this context, a permit is written authorization issued by the town, city or county authorizing construction of a structure on land (ie. house, deck, pool, extension, sunroom, etc). Once the permit is issued and the structure is complete, an inspector from the town, city or county will confirm the structure has been built "to code" and fulfills the requirements of the permit. If so, the town, city or county will issue a certificate of occupancy for the structure.

If a certificate of occupancy does not exist for the house or any structure on the property, the Purchaser should speak with their lender before closing to determine if this will pose any issue obtaining loan approval. The Purchaser, realtor or attorney, should also inquire if the Seller will obtain the certificate of occupancy prior to closing. Even renovated homes with systems that were not installed *to code* may become the new homeowners' responsibility to fix (and finance) if not resolved before closing. In the alternative, many new construction homes come with specific warranties so speak with your realtor or attorney about warranties if you are purchasing a newly constructed home.

I represented a Purchaser who was informed the property would be sold in "as is" condition, and the Seller would not obtain any Certificates of Occupancy for the very large deck in the backyard. She spoke with one lender who informed her that she could only purchase the property with all the proper Certificates of Occupancy. After contacting a different lender, she was informed that so long as there was no open permit for the deck, the mortgage lender would approve the loan without the Seller producing the Certificate of Occupancy.

Before making the offer, always ask if there are any open permits on the home, as this may affect the mortgage approval. If one lender says it will not lend, be sure to speak with another to get a second or third opinion.

Home inspections are even more critical if you are buying a home in "as is" condition. This is often the case on an REO property (also known as "real estate owned" or "bank owned" property) in which the original lender foreclosed on the property and it is now owned by a mortgage lender or bank. The bank has already lost money due to the foreclosure and does not wish to place any more money in the property to perform renovations. In this case, the bank will list the property in "as is" condition and a Purchaser will be responsible for any repairs after closing. Similarly, short sales or homes held in the name of an Estate and Trust are often sold in an "as is" condition, so it is wise to complete a home inspection on these types of properties.

Some lenders or loan products will not allow financing on homes without a home inspection as some homes can be deemed uninsurable due to potentially life-threatening issues like mold, radon, carbon monoxide issues, or faulty wiring that can cause fires. For instance, a recent client wanted to purchase a home that not only had a fire, but the firemen flooded the home while putting out the fire. No lender would touch the house, and no company would provide homeowners' insurance. Not only did the Seller have to sell the house much lower than it would normally sell for, but the Purchaser who really wanted the house had no choice but to pay cash for it. He later remodeled the home and refinanced it to recoup his cash. Of course, not everyone is in the position to buy a home without mortgage financing and complete renovations, but this example shows that there is a buyer for every home, regardless of its condition.

Is It Smart to Buy a Home without an Inspection?

This quick answer is NO. The failure to obtain a proper home inspection conducted by a licensed professional can result in a loss of time and money, and we know how valuable both are during your homeownership journey. Choose wisely.

Be sure to proceed with caution if you decide to purchase a home without completing a home inspection. In a Seller's market, when the demand is high and there are multiple

Purchasers, waiving an inspection increases your chances of securing your new home. However, this is extremely risky, as it could put you at a huge financial risk in the long run by potentially blindsiding you with unexpected repairs.

There have been many circumstances where a Purchaser waived their inspection only to have to replace boilers or hot water heaters in the winter or flooded basements every time it rains. Particularly in the summer months, you may discover the air conditioning unit is broken and the pool has inadequate filtration systems, all of which could have been discovered through the inspection and repaired by the Seller prior to closing. Choosing to waive the inspection can cost thousands of dollars, as we know all of these systems are costly.

One Purchaser absolutely refused to hire a licensed home inspector because the home was newly renovated. Against my advice and the advice of her realtor, she decided to have a family member that "bought numerous homes" act as the inspector. On her first night in the house, she heard what sounded like multiple people running through the home. She believed someone had broken into the house. When she turned on the light, the noise stopped. This happened for several nights (not sure how she fell asleep each night).

She finally decided to hire a licensed inspector to determine the cause of the noise.

The inspector found that the entire house was infested with rats, as indicated by droppings in hidden places throughout the home. So when she turned off the lights each night, the rats would come out to play. After further inspection, it was found the rats had caused significant damage to the home, causing the Purchaser to pay for exterminator costs and new insulation. The inspector even discovered that the electrical throughout the house was incorrectly wired, which could cause a fire. If the homebuyer had completed a home inspection with a licensed professional prior to closing, the costs to remedy this could have been presented to the Seller for a possible reduction of the purchase price or remedy before closing.

Be sure to hire a licensed home inspector even if the home appears to be in good condition.

Inspections should always be top priority when purchasing a home, though there are cases when they can be waived. Below are some questions that you should know before moving forward with or without an inspection:

1. What is the purpose of a home inspection?
2. Does the Purchaser or Seller order the home inspection?
3. Is a home inspection mandatory?
4. Who do you need to contact for a home inspection?
5. Should you waive an inspection, even in a "hot market"?

CHAPTER 6

Congrats! Your Offer Has Been Accepted. Now What?

Time to Hire an Attorney

You have made an offer on a home, and your offer has been accepted. Congrats! Perhaps your inspection has been complete (or scheduled), and now it is time to sign a contract.

So what is a real estate contract, and why is it important?

A real estate contract is a legally binding agreement between two or more competent parties (Purchaser and Seller) which contains the agreed-upon terms of the purchase/sale of a piece of property (residential or commercial).

Your real estate contract should contain the purchase price, property address, contractual down payment, any contingency clauses, proposed closing date, and any other provisions that may be unique to your purchase of this particular property (i.e., repairs). Anything that was agreed to verbally with the Seller or their realtor must be included in the written real estate contract.

In most states, a real estate contract must be written to be enforceable. All provisions included in the written contract should hold the other party liable for its performance. If it is not in writing, it was not agreed upon, as you do not have written proof of the verbal conversation and promise. Oral agreements of real estate terms are not enforceable (or legally binding) until they are memorialized in a signed agreement, called a contract of sale.

Remember this, as there have been many instances where a Purchaser failed to disclose a verbal conversation that took place with the Seller concerning the home. Often, the Seller will agree to delivery and installation of a washer and dryer, for example, and on the day of closing, deny the promise was ever made.

On one occasion, a Purchaser and Seller had a verbal one-to-one conversation during the home inspection, unbeknownst to either realtor. This is unusual, but the Purchaser and Seller knew each other through mutual friends. The Seller informed the Purchaser that he would leave all of the TVs, the tools in the shed, and the lawnmower and promised to remove the non-working washer and dryer and install a brand-new washer and dryer. The Seller also promised to fix the leak under the kitchen sink.

When reviewing the contract with the Purchaser, the attorney asked, "Did the Seller make any verbal promises to repair, replace or include any items as part of the transaction?" to which the Purchaser responded "No," because he felt that this information was unimportant. The verbal representation of the Seller was never placed in the contract, and neither the realtors nor the attorney were made aware of this conversation. On the day of closing, the Purchaser completed a walk-through of the premises and discovered all TVs were removed along with the tools, lawnmower, washer, and dryer. The leak under the kitchen sink was not fixed, and the new washer and dryer were not purchased by the Seller.

When the Purchaser asked the Seller about the whereabouts of these items, the Seller indicated that he did not recall having this conversation with the Purchaser and therefore was not responsible for producing these items. If there was a written agreement put in place and signed by both parties, the Purchaser could have held the Seller in default of the agreement. However, since nothing was placed in writing, the Seller was not responsible. The Purchaser's attorney was able to enter into an Escrow agreement to ensure the Seller hired a licensed plumber to repair the leak after closing, as standard contract language covered this. However, the Purchaser was left to purchase his own TVs, tools, and lawnmower, which cost him much more than he anticipated.

A simple update to the contract could have prevented this and saved the Purchaser money and time.

You absolutely do not want to be disappointed on the day of your closing, assuming the Seller has completed something that was discussed several months prior but was never memorialized in signed writing: a real estate contract.

As we will discuss in detail in Chapter 8, a walk-through of the premises is completed on the day of closing. This allows the Purchaser to confirm the property is vacant, broom swept, and otherwise in the condition required under the contract of sale. At this time, the Purchaser may notice that a repair item that was included in the contract was not completed by the Seller,

In this case, the Seller may have forgotten their contractual responsibility to complete the repair before closing, either intentionally or unintentionally (we will give them the benefit of the doubt here). On the bright side, you can now enforce the provision of the contract that requires the Seller to complete the repair, as you were sure this promise was included in the written contract, at the onset of the transaction. Therefore, the repair must be completed by the Seller, even if done so after closing.

Another example is if the Seller removes an item that was promised in the signed contract of sale. Suppose the contract indicates the chandelier in the dining room will remain. In that case, the Seller can be held liable for removing this item from the home.

Both parties, Seller and Purchaser, are responsible for including all terms of the transaction in the contract by communicating with their real estate attorney, who is trained to include specific language in the contract concerning the transaction. If all pertinent information concerning the transaction is provided to the attorney and the contract is carefully drafted and negotiated, neither party should be left in the dark at closing. It is good practice to consult with a real estate attorney experienced in representing Purchasers and Sellers of the exact type of property you are purchasing, prior to signing any contract.

Do not wait until your offer is accepted to hire your real estate attorney. This may delay the release of the contract of sale by the Seller's counsel or your realtor. Every day that the contract is not signed is an opportunity for another Purchaser to submit a higher offer on the property To reduce potential delays, you must be diligent throughout your home buying journey and also be sure to choose an attorney who is experienced closing transactions on the type of home you are purchasing,

For example, if you are purchasing a cooperative apartment or a multifamily home, you want to be sure your selected attorney handles these types of transactions. There could be small nuances on these property types that your attorney should be aware of. A small misstep can cause a significant delay.

It is strongly recommended that your attorney has experience in handling real estate transactions. As we discuss throughout the book, your team is very important and can make or break your deal. If you hire a criminal attorney, for example, they may be more than capable of representing you in your real estate transaction but have limited time to answer your question while on a criminal trial or lack the experience to resolve a complicated title issue, causing a significant delay in closing.

An attorney with a focus on transactional real estate will understand the strict timeframes which the parties must adhere to in a contract and will do what they can to ensure they are available to review the contract with you quickly, upon receipt, to help ensure you do not lose the property to a higher offer.

This is an important point because, often, a Purchaser may believe that a verbal acceptance of your offer to purchase is enough to "lock in" the Seller. However, as discussed, a real estate contract ***must*** be signed by both Purchaser and Seller to be deemed enforceable. Therefore, a Purchaser can sign a contract and provide a contractual down payment, and the Seller can still take a higher offer before signing your contract. There is nothing a Purchaser can do at this point but to either match or outbid the offer. The Seller was not "locked in" because the contract had not been fully executed by both parties.

Remember, even though your offer has been accepted, you are not "in a contract" until both parties have signed the contract and you have tendered your contractual deposit.

When hiring an attorney to work with you through closing, it may be valuable to ask if they have an assistant, paralegal, or a team of paralegals who work with them to ensure the transaction moves smoothly and without delay. Even if the attorney does not attend court, they may be unable to answer the phone or an email until after hours, if in closings throughout the workday. In addition, an attorney may have back-to-back closings (which may take approximately two hours per closing to complete). An attorney with an assistant, paralegal, or team of paralegals can keep the engine running even while the attorney is in a closing, engaged with a client, or on vacation.

Stay engaged with the process where you can. You are purchasing a home and do not want any unnecessary delays. Ask questions throughout the transaction as they may arise. Make sure you understand the reason for a delay, what happens next, what to bring to closing, etc.

There are times when there is an emergency situation that must be resolved immediately. For example, your lender may realize that your mortgage rate is due to expire at the end of the week. Therefore, you will need to close before the rate expires. You want to be able to reach out to your attorney and/or their team of paralegals, who will quickly contact all parties to begin the scheduling process. A one-day delay could cause unnecessary strain on your transaction. What if something happens on a holiday or weekend? Does your attorney provide their cell phone number or instructions if an emergency situation were to arise after hours? Be sure to ask the right questions when choosing a real estate attorney.

Not all states require an attorney to represent the Purchaser or Seller in a real estate transaction. However, you are engaging in one of the most important transactions of your life, so it is a good idea to have one on your side. Remember, you are signing a legally binding contract containing terms that may be difficult to interpret. In the states that require and/or strongly encourage an attorney to represent a Purchaser, the Purchaser's counsel generally reviews and submits comments to the contract drafted by the Seller's counsel. In turn, the Seller's counsel will approve, deny, or negotiate the provisions requested by the Purchaser's counsel.

The role of your real estate attorney is to ensure you are legally protected when you purchase a home. An experienced real estate attorney is generally trained to understand and interpret the contractual provisions, the laws governing real estate in your jurisdiction, and the customary language which should appear in your real estate contract.

Your real estate attorney should explain the contract to you in a way that you can understand and feel comfortable in moving forward with the transaction. If you are uncomfortable with the attorney or the contractual provisions, you may be more hesitant to tender your contractual down payment at the onset of the transaction or move forward with signing the contract. Never be afraid to adjust and communicate if you ever feel uncomfortable throughout the transaction. You must choose an attorney you can relate to and trust to walk you through the process. Hiring an experienced and relatable attorney will make the transaction smoother and help lessen your potential stress levels.

Typically, the release of the contract deposit is the most difficult part for a first-time homebuyer. The contractual deposit is often the largest lump sum that an individual has ever paid in their lifetime. However, your attorney is there to protect you and your down payment, so be sure to trust the process and do not stress over those things you have little control over, such as a slight Seller delay in scheduling the closing.

Your attorney will also be a liaison between all parties. This is the individual who will be best equipped to set expectations for you throughout the transaction. On average, you are on this journey with your attorney for approximately

60 to 90 days, depending on the terms of your transaction. Your attorney may become your confidante throughout the transaction, and you should share any concerns you have. Remember, you have attorney/client privilege, so your conversations with your attorney should remain confidential. Don't be afraid to express yourself through closing. Sometimes a real estate transaction is a great test of patience and stamina, so stay in it until the end and do not give up!

Here are some important questions you should ask your real estate attorney before hiring them:

1. What is your experience handling real estate transactions?
2. Is real estate your primary practice area? Will you be in a trial when it is time to review the contract? What happens if you are on vacation when it's time to schedule a closing?
3. Do you work with a team of paralegals? Will I be able to get my questions answered if you are unavailable?
4. Do you have time to take on my transaction? Have you reached capacity?
5. How will you receive payment? Flat fee? Hourly? Payment at closing or prior?
6. What are your office hours? Is email, cell, or office phone the best and quickest form of communication?

CHAPTER 7

We Have the Contract, What's Next?

Once the Seller's counsel or the realtor prepares the contract, your role is to review and understand the provisions contained within the document *before* signing. If you hire an attorney, they will interpret the contract provisions and explain them to you in terms you can understand. DO NOT SIGN ANYTHING THAT YOU DO NOT UNDERSTAND OR DO NOT AGREE WITH.

The day you sign your contract is a day you will never forget. This is a big moment for anyone, particularly a first-time homebuyer! You may experience a range of emotions, including excitement, nervousness, fear, as well as an undeniable sense of accomplishment.

Remember, you have chosen an all-star team which includes your attorney, mortgage banker, and realtor who will be there with you to provide support all the way to the closing table. This is truly a life-changing moment that you have worked so hard to achieve. Capture the moment by taking pictures and video chat with a family member after you have signed the contract, so they can celebrate with you. I once represented a Purchaser who had a professional photographer come to the contract signing because she wanted to capture this moment for her family who lived out of state. She dressed to impress—hair, makeup—and brought her special pen to the contract signing. She told me that she had doubted herself for a long time and wanted to document her progress to be an example to her family and friends that if she could do it, they could too!

This is a moment to take a deep breath and congratulate yourself for getting here. It's time, no turning back.

As your experienced real estate attorney explains all the provisions on the contract, you want to take notes as to important dates, which are usually deadlines to complete a certain tasks and your responsibilities through closing.

Mortgage Contingency 101

The mortgage contingency date is the deadline to provide the Seller's counsel with a mortgage commitment letter. This date should be marked on your calendar. It is an integral part of the deal, and if it is not delivered on time, it can cause the Seller to cancel the contract and even retain the contract deposit. It is pertinent that you understand all of the contract terms, to not unintentionally miss a deadline. You must be aware of your responsibilities under the contract you sign.

What Happens on Closing Day?

Another important date in your real estate contract will be the closing date. You certainly do not want to miss this date by misunderstanding what it means to close "on," "on or before," OR "on or about" a specified date that may appear in the contract.

As I want you to be a step ahead, note the following closing date representations:

ON - Closing date "on" January 1. This means the closing will be scheduled for the specified date as stated, January 1.

ON OR BEFORE - Closing date "on or before" January 1. This means the closing must take place any day before January 1 or on the specified date as stated, January 1.

ON OR ABOUT - Closing date "on or about" January 1. This means the closing must take place on any date before, on, or within 30 days *after* the specified closing date. In other words, the last date to close would be February 1.

Frequently Asked Questions

There are a few big questions that clients often ask. I'd like to break those questions down so you can have a head start on what to expect. Note, this information does not establish an attorney-client relationship, and this is for informational purposes only.

What Happens If I Do Not Qualify for a Mortgage?

This is one of the most-asked questions from our first-time homebuyers, and justifiably so. This is where the mortgage contingency clause in your contract comes into play. The mortgage contingency clause generally allows a specific timeframe (say, 30 days) for the Purchaser to obtain a mortgage commitment from their mortgage lender. If the Purchaser is denied a mortgage within this timeframe, the mortgage denial letter must be produced, and if there is no contractual default on the Purchaser's end, the deposit is returned to the Purchaser, and the contract is canceled. Once canceled, there shall be no further responsibilities of either party, and the Seller can re-list the property and sell it to another Purchaser. The mortgage contingency clause is one of the most important clauses in your contract if you are applying for financing when purchasing a home.

What Happens If the Appraisal Comes Back Low?

A mortgage lender generally requires an appraisal to be completed before the issuance of a mortgage commitment. This is because the lender wants to be sure there is enough value in the property to substantiate the loan amount offered, as compared to the contractual purchase price. Therefore, the lender will hire an independent appraiser to complete the appraisal and give the home a particular value.

In other words, the appraiser will determine what the house is worth based on several factors, such as square footage, location, condition of the property, recent sales of comparable properties, etc. If the appraisal is returned at a price that is lower than the contract price, the lender will likely decrease the loan amount, which will require the Purchaser to bring more money to the closing table to complete the transaction. Notwithstanding a contractual clause to the contrary, a Purchaser will request the Seller reduce their purchase price to match the property's appraised value.

The Seller can decide to reduce the price to the appraised value (or a number close, requiring the Purchaser to bring the difference to closing) or cancel the contract (if the Purchaser does not have the funds or does not wish to pay the difference). If the Seller refuses to reduce the purchase price and decides to cancel the contract, the Purchaser is entitled to the return of the contract deposit unless a clause in the contract states otherwise. Please be sure to discuss any appraisal provisions with your attorney before signing the contract.

What Happens If the Seller Cannot Provide a House with Clear Title?

When you purchase a home, you generally do not want to take on the debts and financial responsibilities of the Seller. You also want to ensure that you are purchasing the home from its rightful owner. This is why it is important for your attorney to order a title report from a reputable title company. The title report will reflect the true ownership of the property and any liens, judgments, open permits, violations, etc., associated with the home. Your attorney's role is to work with the Seller's counsel and the title company to ensure these items are resolved prior to closing (or, in some cases, after) so that you are purchasing a home with a clean title. The last thing you want, is to close on a home and have the Seller's mortgage lender serve you with a foreclosure notice because you purchased a home with an outstanding mortgage!

To use this as an example: If the Seller applied for a mortgage on the home, this mortgage must be paid in full at closing. The title company, through its representative, will collect the check needed to satisfy the mortgage in full (generally, this comes from the Seller's closing proceeds) and will forward the check to the mortgage company. Once the mortgage company receives the check, a satisfaction of the mortgage will be returned to the title company for recording, and the lien is removed off the record. This is an instance where the lien is officially removed after closing.

Other title issues which can appear on the title report are open permits, wherein the Seller may have applied for a permit with the city/town/county to complete work on the property and failed to schedule an inspection with the city/town/county to ensure the work was completed to code. This can significantly delay a closing if not quickly discovered and resolved by the Seller. If you choose to hire an attorney, the attorney can assist with negotiations. For example, if offered a credit on the purchase price, a Purchaser may decide to purchase the property with the open item title matter. In the alternative, money can be held in the Seller's escrow account post-closing until such time as the Seller remedies the condition.

If there is a title issue that cannot be resolved by the Seller, there is typically a provision in the contract which allows the Seller to cancel the contract and return the Purchaser's deposit. Though rare, this could arise if there is a monetary judgment or outstanding mortgage against the premises and not enough money in the sale of the home to cover satisfaction of the Seller's lien/judgment.

The title report and title insurance are invaluable when purchasing a home. Once the contract of sale is fully executed, the title report is ordered by Purchaser's counsel. The title matters which appear throughout the report are resolved by the attorneys and/or Seller or Purchaser and once cleared, the title company will provide a title insurance policy at closing. This policy is provided to a Purchaser at the

Closing table and if title has been cleared by the parties at or prior to closing, the policy will reflect no outstanding matters such as liens or judgments, attached to the premises. This title insurance policy becomes extremely important when you decide to later sell your property as it shows the state of title at the time of purchase. The last thing you want is to purchase a home and be left with the financial and legal responsibilities of the prior owner. Therefore, due diligence, a thorough review of the title report and issuance of the title insurance policy, is important in your journey to homeownership.

How Will We Go into the Title? What If Something Happens to Me?

At the closing table, the title closer will ask: "How would you like to take title?" In other words, if the Purchaser buys a home with 2 or more parties, what happens with the interest in the property when a party dies? The deed should reflect proper title so that the parties do not run into issues when it is time to sell the home. Real property can be held (titled) in one of three ways when there are two or more Purchasers/owners: Tenants in common, Joint Tenants with Rights of Survivorship, or Tenancy by the entirety.

Now I know these terms may seem complicated, but here is a simple breakdown.

Tenants in common:

This is when two or more parties hold a portion of the property, generally a 50/50 percentage interest (or some other variation of a fractional interest). If one of the parties were to die prior to the sale of the premises, that party's interest in the property would be held in the person's Estate. If the surviving party decides to later sell the property, they must coordinate with the representative/fiduciary appointed for the Estate, as the Estate is entitled to its share of the closing proceeds. There are no survivorship rights when the title is held as tenants in common. If the deed is silent as to how two parties will hold title to the premises, it is generally assumed the intent was a 50/50 split as tenants in common.

Joint Tenants with Rights of Survivorship:

This is when two or more parties hold title to the premises, generally in equal shares. In the case of the death of one of the individuals, their remaining interests pass in their entirety to the surviving owner. The deed should state the names of the new owners with a notation "as joint tenants with rights of survivorship" in order to be effective. Many family members hold title this way to avoid a lengthy probate proceeding in the surrogate's court appointing a legal representative for the Estate, in the case of the death of one of the parties. In other words, the surviving party can immediately sell the property in the case of the other owner's death without waiting for an Administrator or Executor to be appointed to the Estate.

Tenants by the entirety:

When a husband and wife purchase a home, they customarily hold title as tenants by the entirety, which is a form of ownership reserved for married couples. Similar to joint tenants with rights of survivorship, in the case of the death of one of the spouses, the home is vested completely in the surviving spouse. If the intent is for the parties to hold the title as tenants by the entirety, the deed should specifically state this or in the alternative "as husband and wife."

If you are purchasing a home, whether on your own or with multiple individuals, it is good practice to have a will in place that specifies the intent of the home after death and ensure the appropriate language is included in your deed at closing. If you are ever unsure, speak with the title representative or your attorney, who will guide you at the closing table.

What Happens If the Seller Defaults under the Contract?

Though rare, a Seller may wake up one morning and decide they no longer want to sell their home. It would be deemed a default for either a Purchaser or Seller to take such a stance after the contract has been signed by both parties.

At this point, the Seller can return the down payment, of course, if the Purchaser is in agreement to cancel the contract. However, that is not usually the case for a Purchaser who had their heart fixed on a property that the Seller now refuses to sell. In this case, there is a legal remedy for the Purchaser in what is called "specific performance." Your attorney should ensure this provision is a remedy in the contract you sign at the start of the transaction.

The specific performance provision means that if the Seller does not perform based on the contract's provisions, the Seller is now in default, and the Purchaser has a right to start a lawsuit. In a lawsuit for specific performance, a

Purchaser will produce a copy of the contract to the court explaining that the Seller withdrew their promise to sell the property. Depending on the circumstances of the Seller, the court may likely require the Seller to perform under the contract and sell the premises as promised, and, this time, under court order!

Remember, it is important to hire an experienced real estate attorney to review the provisions of the contract with you so that You, Too, Can Be a Homeowner (with legal backup through your journey!)

CHAPTER 8

Your Final Walk-Through

A real estate contract generally allows a Purchaser to complete a walk-through of the property sometime within 48 hours before closing. The final walk-through is the Purchaser's last chance to view and inspect the property before taking ownership of their new home.

The purpose of the walk-through is to ensure that the Sellers have complied with all of their responsibilities concerning the delivery of the property on closing day. For example, most standard real estate contracts require the Sellers to leave the house in "broom swept" condition. This means the property is clean, swept and the kitchen and bathrooms have been maintained. In addition, the Sellers must leave behind anything they agreed will remain pursuant to the contract and remove those items considered personal belongings and/or debris (junk).

Unless the contract states otherwise, it is generally not required to hire a cleaning service to complete a thorough cleaning of the property. Still, all personal belongings and debris should be removed from the home. Unless otherwise agreed, the appliances and fixtures should remain at the property, and all should remain in working order, including plumbing, heating, air conditioning, and electrical systems. The Seller is usually responsible for extensive damage to walls or fixtures affected during the move-out process.

Often the Purchaser will view the premises solely with their realtor. Occasionally, however, and under certain circumstances, the Purchaser may bring in the inspector who completed the inspection at the start of the transaction. For example, the Purchaser may bring the home inspector to the walk-through if there are major repair items on the repair rider and the Purchaser wants to ensure that the work was properly completed by a licensed professional, as promised by the Seller under the repair provision in the contract.

The Purchaser's role at the walk-through is solely to ensure the house is in substantially the same condition from when you initially conducted your home inspection and the repairs stated in the contract, if any, have been completed.

There have been many times a Purchaser was so excited to close that they did not do a thorough walk-through of the home prior to closing.

Once the closing is scheduled, I always remind the Purchaser to complete not just a drive-by of the property but thoroughly walk through the home (closets, attic, and shed included) to confirm that the property is vacant, broom swept, and all plumbing, heating, air conditioning and electrical are in working order.

Sometimes the Purchaser does a walk-through and may forget to turn on the shower, only to discover that it does not work several days after the closing, once they move into the property. In the alternative, the shed is completely filled with the Seller's garbage which is now the Purchaser's responsibility to remove.

The time it takes to do a walk-through varies depending on the size of the house and how much time you wish to spend, to complete a *thorough* inspection of the home. It can take twenty minutes for smaller houses or more than an hour. It is up to you. Give yourself time to check the entire home. There is no need to rush or feel rushed. You want to be sure there are no surprises when moving in. It's important to double- and triple-check everything in the home during your walk-through. You will be glad you took the time to do it right.

The final walk-through should be as close to the closing date and time as possible. In my opinion, taking the day off from work is always the best option, so you do not have to rush through the day. You also want to see the property right before you arrive at the closing table.

Completing the walk-through on the morning of the closing also allows the Seller time to remove all of their possessions from the home so the Purchaser can view the premises while vacant. Often the Seller will hire a moving company to arrive the night before or morning of the closing. If you go to the house the night before, the Sellers' moving trucks may be at the premises, obstructing your view of certain areas of the home while boxes are being removed.

It is best to see the property when it is vacant and free of all of the Seller's personal belongings. If a Purchaser does a walk-through while boxes are layered in the living room, for example, you may miss the large hole in the wall from the removal of the TV (which should have been repaired by the Seller before closing) or forget to turn on and check the lights on a sunny day since access to the light switches are blocked.

Ideally, on the day of closing, you will wake up refreshed, do your walk-through, stop at the bank to get your certified check, bring your personal checkbook and two forms of identification, and make your way to the closing. By the time you make it to closing, you have completed a day's work, and this is the finale! Don't forget, though, you have a team with you every step of the way. Your realtor will be there with you at the walk-through, and your attorney will happily wait for you at the closing table and answer any questions throughout. Be sure to make childcare arrangements, notify your employer, and allow yourself adequate travel time. This is your big day, so don't be late!

Unfortunately, things can happen during the Seller's move-out process or while the house sits vacant leading up to closing. The Seller may have overlooked some repair items or failed to remove personal items from a shed or garage. If you find such issues on your walk-through, speak with your realtor or attorney. We are there to resolve these matters as they arise.

Never ever skip the final walk-through, no matter the circumstances. I recently represented a Purchaser who was informed the walk-through could only be completed virtually. This is not ideal and mostly unacceptable. You cannot ensure the heat in the home kicks on virtually. There are just some things you will need to see and feel in person when completing a walk-through.

I represented a Purchaser who agreed to buy a house with a tenant for investment purposes. On the day of closing, the realtor was informed that the Purchaser would not be given access to the property to complete a walk-through because the tenant was not feeling well. Instead, the Seller asked the tenant to walk through the house with his phone to capture the condition of the premises. Though the video could show that the house is still standing and the water comes on, a video cannot prove that the water turns hot or cold, or the heat kicks on and actually feels hot. When doing a walk-through, the Purchaser should be able to visit the property personally, as this is the last opportunity before closing to discuss the condition of the property with the Seller.

Once you close, the house is yours, and any unresolved issue then becomes the Purchaser's responsibility. Therefore, a Purchaser must address any problems with the Seller *before* closing.

A Purchaser should have their inspection report and the repair rider to the contract, if any, at the time of the walk-through. This is not an opportunity to ask the Seller to repair items that were already raised in the initial inspection. Those repairs should have been completed and signed off by now. This is the time to ensure the property is vacant and broom swept and all personal belongings and debris have been removed from the premises.

Bring a pen and notepad—or your phone—to take notes. Take pictures if there are any conditions you need to raise at closing. Additionally, bring a working charger to check the electrical outlets. You may want to write a list of items you wish to check before your walk-through so that you do not forget anything. There will be a lot going on this day, so do not leave anything to memory.

In speaking with a colleague, I was told the story of a client who felt something was not right with some black stains he saw around the carpet; it was only on the home's second floor. No one seemed to have any answers as to why they were there. After much resistance, the Seller agreed to issue a credit to the Purchaser for the condition of the carpet which was not in this condition at the time of the initial offer or home inspection.

After closing, the Purchaser decided to have the carpets steamed to see if the stains would come out. In conversation with the steaming company, one of the professionals mentioned that he'd been at the house a few months prior and there had been a fire in the house. The previous sellers had renovated only the damaged areas and did not disclose the fire.

The Purchaser certainly was not expecting to hear this and informed his attorney. As the Seller provided a credit at the closing, any remaining repairs would be the Purchaser's responsibility, as the new owner of the home.

If there are any issues discovered during the walk-through, the Seller can offer a credit to the Purchaser to cover the costs to hire a licensed professional, to make the repairs. Another option is for Seller's counsel (or the title company) to hold money in escrow from the Seller's proceeds, until such time as the repair is resolved by a licensed professional, after Closing.

The Purchaser and/or Seller can obtain quotes from a licensed professional who will determine the costs, and the Purchaser and Seller can negotiate a credit (or escrow amount) that will make the parties comfortable in moving forward to Closing. Negotiations are typically done through either the real estate agents or attorneys trained to come to an amicable solution.

If a solution cannot be reached, which is extremely rare, a Purchaser can request an adjournment of the closing until the repairs can be completed. In even rarer cases, the Purchaser may want to back out of the deal if an agreement cannot be reached. As the Seller wants to sell and the Purchaser wants to buy, it is unusual to have significant walk-through issues that cannot be resolved at the final stretch.

The day of the walk-through is generally an exciting day for all parties and one of the last stages of your homeownership journey. Congratulations for making it this far, and see you at the closing table!

Walk-throughs are extremely important so do not skip this step. Below are some questions to answer before completing your walk-through:

1. When should the final walk-through take place?
2. List items to bring to the walk-through.
3. Is the Seller still responsible for anything before closing?
4. Who should you contact if a problem arises?

CHAPTER 9

Welcome to the Closing Table

Real Estate Closings 101

If you made it this far, it's certainly time to start the pre-party, but do not stay up too late the night before and miss the main attraction: The Closing Table!

On the day of closing, you may experience mixed emotions. After all, you have made it through one of the biggest achievements of your life. You have accomplished something for you and your family that will now change the trajectory of your life and the generations to come. This is big. Do not take this day for granted, and watch how your emotions begin to tilt towards happiness and gratitude.

Your realtor, attorney, and mortgage lender might have mentioned your closing day throughout the process, but no one discusses what happens on this day (until it is scheduled). Well, by reading this book, you will be one step ahead of the average Purchaser! Closing day will not be a mysterious or intimidating event; it should be treated like the grand finale of your journey. Finally, you have made it to the finish line.

Closing day marks the official transfer of the title of the property from Seller to Purchaser. This is evidenced by the signing of the deed by the Seller showing that the property has been delivered to you. You and/or your attorney and/or the title company will double-check the deed to ensure it contains the correct spelling of your name (including middle initials, if any) and it matches your name as reflected on the mortgage. If you are purchasing the home with a spouse, you want to ensure the deed references both names with a notation, "as husband and wife," or "tenants by the entirety." If you are purchasing with a family member or friend, you want to speak with your attorney about various ways to hold title such as "tenants in common" or "joint tenants with rights of survivorship."

As discussed in Chapter 7, how Purchasers take title dictates what happens to ownership if one of the parties were to predecease another. Does their right extinguish (joint tenants with right of survivorship) or remain in their Estate (tenants in common)? I suggest you seek the advice of counsel in your jurisdiction before your closing date when making this decision.

Depending on your state, you will sign documents at the closing table with a title company, representative of your lender, OR attorney, who will explain the terms contained within the closing documents. If you have applied for a mortgage, you want to ensure you are informed of your mortgage payment, your first date of payment, grace period, interest rate (fixed or variable, and if variable, when will it change), and any other responsibilities you may have under the terms of your mortgage loan.

If you have any questions during the signing, do not be afraid to ask. You should not feel rushed or too uncomfortable to speak up during this process. If any issues arose during the final walk-through of the home, you want to address them before or at the closing table. Do not skip this step out of excitement or lack of time.

Remember, once you sign on the dotted line and receive the keys, the home is yours! Once the closing is complete, there is no going back to request adjustments to your closing documents or the house itself by the Seller.

During the closing, you will review and sign a great deal of documents, so allow yourself at least two hours to complete the closing. If you have work obligations, do your best to set expectations with your employer, sitter, etc., before your closing, so you do not have the added stress of time constraints.

Once your closing is scheduled, you want to make a list of any documentation your attorney, the title company, or your lender requires you to bring. This often includes two forms of valid identification. If your identification is expired, it will not be sufficient, so be sure all of your identification documents are up to date.

Additionally, you may be required to bring a certified check or proof of wire transfer representing your remaining down payment, plus closing costs and any ancillary fees, tips, title closer gratuity, etc. You want to ask your team what is customary in your area as it relates to any title closer gratuity, attorney fees, and the like. In addition to your certified check, bring your checkbook to the closing table. If there is a small adjustment, say ten dollars in the Seller's favor, you typically will need to show this payment in the form of a check rather than cash. Therefore, it is always a good idea to bring your personal checkbook as well, just in case there are any small adjustments made at the closing table.

An example of a small adjustment that could be made at the closing table is for an oil bill. If the home is heated with oil, the Seller will call the oil company prior to closing to read the meter. This way, the Seller will be reimbursed for the oil left in the oil tank. The oil company will advise how many gallons of oil remain in the tank and calculate dollars per gallon. The Seller's counsel may provide the oil reading, for instance, 150 gallons left in the tank at a rate of $2.10/gallon. Thereby the Purchaser must write a check for the sum of $315.00 (150 gallons x $2.10/gallon). Since this adjustment is made at the closing table, after the Purchaser has already tendered the certified check and/or wire transfer, a personal check might be acceptable. This is why it is important to have a checkbook in your possession in case it becomes necessary at closing.

Getting Prepared to Close; Understanding Your Closing Costs

The week before closing can seem like an extremely stressful time. Your closing date is set, and you have an estimate of your closing costs, but not the final numbers. You still have to plan to complete the walk-through, get your certified check, and take off from work—and, quite simply, life is still happening, all while you are about to fulfill a lifelong dream of becoming a homeowner!

Knowing what to expect leading up to the closing is half the battle and can help alleviate stress. Ideally, you should be calm during the days leading up to closing so you can enjoy the journey to the closing table. Finally, you have made it to the final stretch in this marathon!

If you have applied and were approved for a mortgage, your mortgage lender will forward a "Closing Disclosure" to you approximately three days before closing. The closing disclosure will contain the anticipated closing date, the purchase price, loan amount, your interest rate, the names of the borrowers and lender, the mortgage term and loan type, principal and interest payment, escrow payments (and whether your taxes and insurance are made a part of your loan), your mortgage payment, and all bank and title closing costs associated with your purchase.

I urge you to thoroughly review your closing disclosure with your lender to ensure you understand every line item. Often this is the first time you have ever received a six-figure loan. This loan comes with costs and terms, and it is not free! Therefore, you must ensure that you understand the terms of the loan you applied for and the terms associated with it before you arrive at the closing table to execute the loan documents formally.

Throughout your homeownership journey, it is crucial you continuously put money aside, as there may be some unexpected costs associated with the purchase of the home discovered on the final days leading up to closing. The charges most often misunderstood are reimbursement of property taxes and oil due to the Seller.

For instance, if you close on April 28 and the Seller has paid the property taxes on the property through the end of the year, you will be responsible for reimbursing the Seller from the closing date (April 28) through the end of the year (December 31) a prorated amount for the taxes. In another example, suppose the Seller just filled their oil tank with a sum of $551.00 a day before closing. In that case, you will be responsible for refunding the Seller approximately $550 at closing. These charges cannot often be anticipated at the onset of the transaction, so be sure to have a cushion when saving money for your closing costs.

During my years as a real estate attorney, I have witnessed clients scrambling on the day of closing to borrow money from family members and friends to cover these unexpected costs. Do not put yourself in a position like this.

Instead, be transparent with your lender on what you can realistically afford, and be sure you include a cushion in your discussions. Be proactive, courageous, and fearless.

"All our dreams can come true if we have the courage to pursue them." - Walt Disney.

Stay in the Loop

Remember what we talked about in Chapter 1? Teamwork makes the dream work.

Before your closing date, do not be afraid to ask your team of professionals questions. No answer is too intrusive, and there is usually nothing we have not heard before. Your team loves when you ask questions because it helps alleviate stress or confusion on closing day and after. We want your closing experience to be as smooth as possible. There are no wrong questions when you are purchasing a home. Your team is there to help, and we will be there with you through closing.

Purchasers sometimes are afraid to ask questions because they feel like they are asking too much or the questions being asked are silly. The point I want to stress here is, there are no silly questions. Make sure you are asking *all* the questions that come up along the way so that you are informed and not blindsided. Your realtor, loan officer, and attorney can answer all of the questions you may have relating to the closing process.

One of my favorite quotes for a first-time homebuyer is found in "Think and Grow Rich" by the renowned author Napoleon Hill: "You are the master of your destiny. You can influence, direct and control your environment. You can make your life what you want it to be." Remember this and believe it throughout your real estate journey.

Your **WHY** must outweigh any excuse as you pursue your dream of homeownership and, ultimately, any goal in life. I want to leave you with two stories of phenomenal clients who pursued their journey of homeownership despite the challenges they faced. My hope is their journeys will, if nothing else, encourage you and remind you that "You, Too, Can Be a Homeowner."

Ms. Smith, a divorcée and single mom, rented an apartment with her two kids and Tyler, the cat. Though she worked hard, she never really envisioned herself owning a home as a single mother. She and her ex-husband would talk about it during their marriage, but they never really took the time to write down their goals and dreams and plan for it. They did not think about where they would live, what the house would look like on the exterior and interior, save for a down payment, discover what they could afford, how they would feel once they moved into the home, reach out to a mortgage lender or realtor, etc. When they decided to split, she lost all desire to own a home until…

One day, over lunch, a co-worker asked her why she did not own a home. She thought of every excuse, including the fact that she was a single mom and the rent was affordable. Nothing seemed to hold any merit for her co-worker, who was also a single mom with two kids. The co-worker told Ms. Smith that homeownership was the best decision she'd ever made.

Even so, Ms. Smith kept true to her belief that homeownership was not for her and her family until, one day, her daughter came home from school and asked, "Mommy, why can't we live in a house like Amanda? Amanda has her own room and a backyard to play in."

Mommy answered, to her daughter's surprise, "We will get a house soon."

Ms. Smith did not even know where to start, but she wanted to fulfill her promise to her daughter. She decided to create a list of goals for her home buying journey and got organized. She spoke with her children about the type of home they wanted to live in, the costs/benefits of living in various areas pertaining to work and school, and ultimately, what the right fit would be for her family. She asked her parents about her decision to purchase a home, and her dad said, "You will not be able to buy a house without your husband."

Ms. Smith, remembering her daughter (who is her WHY), would not give up despite the doubts placed upon her by her dad. There is a phrase I always use when speaking with my clients: "Don't doubt yourself, because there are plenty of people that will do that for you, and sometimes it is the person closest to you. Your job is to prove them wrong."

Ms. Smith did not give up. She spoke with her co-worker, who recommended a mortgage broker, realtor, real estate agent, home inspector, and attorney. The co-worker loved her team and wanted Ms. Smith to have a similar experience. Ms. Smith reached out to the mortgage lender and was asked to provide her last two years of tax returns, W2s, two months of pay stubs and other proof of income, and social security number so the bank could run her credit and other documents unique to her.

Ms. Smith was surprised to hear that she was preapproved for a home for $600,000.00 with a mortgage amount triple what she was paying for rent. She then reached out to a realtor and discussed the type of home that would be ideal for her family. After several months of searching for a home, her offer was accepted for a home for $400,000.00.

It is important to note that though she was approved for up to $600,000.00, she felt the mortgage payment would be more than she was prepared to handle.

On the day of the home inspection, she took off work, and while walking through the home with the inspector, she got a call from her employer, who explained that he had to let her go. She was devastated, to say the least, and started to panic. She had never been unemployed before and did not know what to do.

She called the mortgage broker, who told her that she could not receive a loan while on unemployment, so she should immediately look for another job. By this time, her desire to purchase the home was unmatched, and nothing could stop her even though the timeframe would be a little longer. She was able to obtain another full-time job and also considered what she could do to create additional income. She would sew for her friends and family in her spare time, so she decided to create a Facebook and Instagram page and post her creations.

To her surprise, people started to ask for items she had never created. During a nationwide pandemic and winter months, they asked for masks with logos for companies (bulk orders), scarfs, hats, and many other items. She enlisted her mom, dad, and children to help when the orders became more than she could handle. She created a corporation and a small business while working full time, allowing the mortgage lender to reassess the two incomes coming in and ultimately approve the mortgage loan.

As a result of her relentless determination and drive, Ms. Smith not only became a homeowner but also a business owner. Focus, perseverance, courage, and determination were the keys to her success. She did not want to let her daughter down (her WHY) and wanted to prove to her parents that she could do it against their doubts. When she received the keys to her new home, she hugged her family tight and said, "We did it."

Another inspiring story is of Mr. and Mrs. Johnson, a married couple who started the journey of homeownership when their apartment caught on fire and they lost everything. Mr. Johnson worked as an NYC police officer, and Mrs. Johnson as a school nurse. Both made a decent income but did not have any savings to put money down on a home. They were just starting the process to save the 3.5% they needed for the down payment when disaster struck. A candle in one of the neighboring apartments caused a five-alarm fire in the building, and all of their personal belongings were unsalvageable. They lost it all and had to start from the beginning. They stayed with family and friends and slept on couches.

However, they did not give up on their dream to become homeowners, and both decided that they would work for a ride-sharing company during their days off from their primary jobs. Mr. and Mrs. Johnson worked seven days a week for six months straight. They did not take one day off during this time and held each other accountable. When one wanted to give up, the other reminded them of the end goal. They read and listened to motivational books and podcasts. When the Sellers handed them the keys, they cried tears of joy. We all did.

A positive mindset brings positive results. Mr. and Mrs. Johnson set their mind to achieve a goal, and now, they are homeowners.

These are just two amazing success stories and I want you to be one of them. You, Too, Can Be a Homeowner if you set a goal, follow the information in this book, and never give up.

See you at the closing table! I cannot wait to hear all about your journey.

Made in the USA
Monee, IL
05 November 2026

67379321R00073